MEGA DINOSAURS
CONTENTS

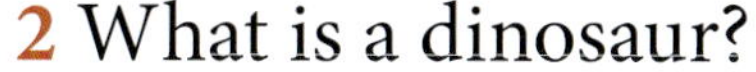

2 What is a dinosaur?
4 Finding dinosaur bones
6 Where did Australian dinosaurs live?
8 Footprints
10 What did they look like?
12 Sauropods
14 *Diamantinasaurus*
16 Theropods
18 *Australovenator*
20 Armoured dinosaurs
22 *Kunbarrasaurus*
24 Ornithopods
26 *Leaellynasaura*
28 Flying and swimming reptiles
30 Glossary

AF583947

WHAT IS A DINOSAUR?

Dinosaurs lived between 245 and 65 million years ago. Some were as big as a two-storey house; others were as small as chickens. Dinosaurs can be placed into two groups – ornithischians and saurischians.

DID YOU KNOW?

All dinosaurs walked on the land. Flying reptiles and swimming reptiles – even the ones that lived at the same time as the dinosaurs – are not dinosaurs.

AUSTRALIAN DINOSAURS

So far, dinosaur experts have identified about 24 different dinosaur species from Australia.

Saurischians are known as 'lizard-hipped' dinosaurs because their hips are similar to the lizards we know today. All carnivorous (meat-eating) dinosaurs fell into this category, including the famous *Tyrannosaurus rex*.

Ornithischians are also called 'bird-hipped' dinosaurs because the structure of their lower body is similar to that of birds. These dinosaurs were herbivores, which means they only ate plants.

DID YOU KNOW?

Dinosaurs are usually known by their scientific name, which is always written in slanted text.

FINDING DINOSAUR BONES

The scientists who search for evidence of dinosaurs are called palaeontologists. When a palaeontologist finds a dinosaur bone, they carefully dig it out of the dirt. Some bones can easily break, so the scientists need to be very careful.

AMMONITE FOSSIL

Even though many dinosaur fossils found in Australia are quite small, palaeontologists can tell a lot about the creature they once belonged to. These scientists can describe a whole dinosaur from just a few small parts, such as a jawbone or tooth.

Pieces of ancient life that we find today are called **FOSSILS**. In most cases fossils don't contain actual bone, but the shape of the bone has been replaced with rock. Fossils can also be the remains of plants, the footsteps of an animal, or even ancient animal poo!

EXPOSING A SAUROPOD SKELETON

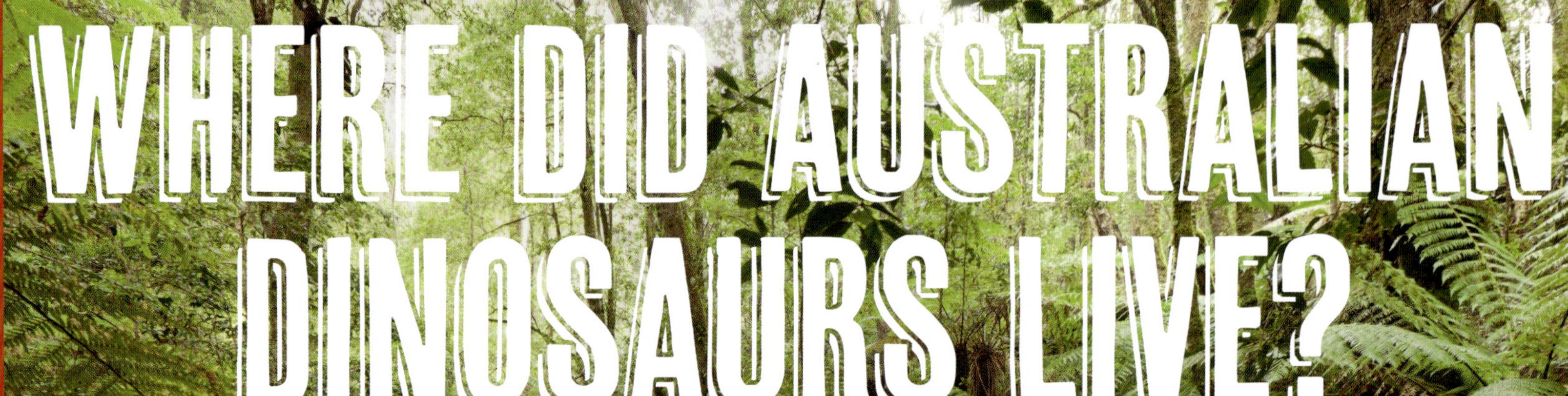

WHERE DID AUSTRALIAN DINOSAURS LIVE?

Dinosaur bones and footprints have been found in all states of Australia. Some key dinosaur sites include Winton in QLD, Broome in WA, Lightning Ridge in NSW and Andamooka in SA.

Dinosaurs found in places like Victoria, such as *Leaellynasaura*, may have lived in **WETLANDS**, surrounded by rivers.

Dinosaurs found in places like Queensland, such as *Muttaburrasaurus*, would have lived in forests filled with ferns and conifers. Ferns are some of the oldest plants on Earth. They lived long before the dinosaurs and still survive today. Conifers look like Christmas trees, and they can grow up to 100m tall.

Some plant species that existed during the time of the dinosaurs still survive today. In Australia, these ancient plants, such as Wollemi pines, are found in rainforests along the eastern coast and in Tasmania.

Most of the dinosaurs that have been found in Australia lived during the **CRETACEOUS PERIOD**. The country looked very different back then. An inland sea stretched across Australia, through what is now Queensland and South Australia.

In Lightning Ridge, NSW, fossils are preserved in a material called **OPAL**. They are usually found by miners digging deep into the ground. These fossils can be brightly coloured and very beautiful to look at.

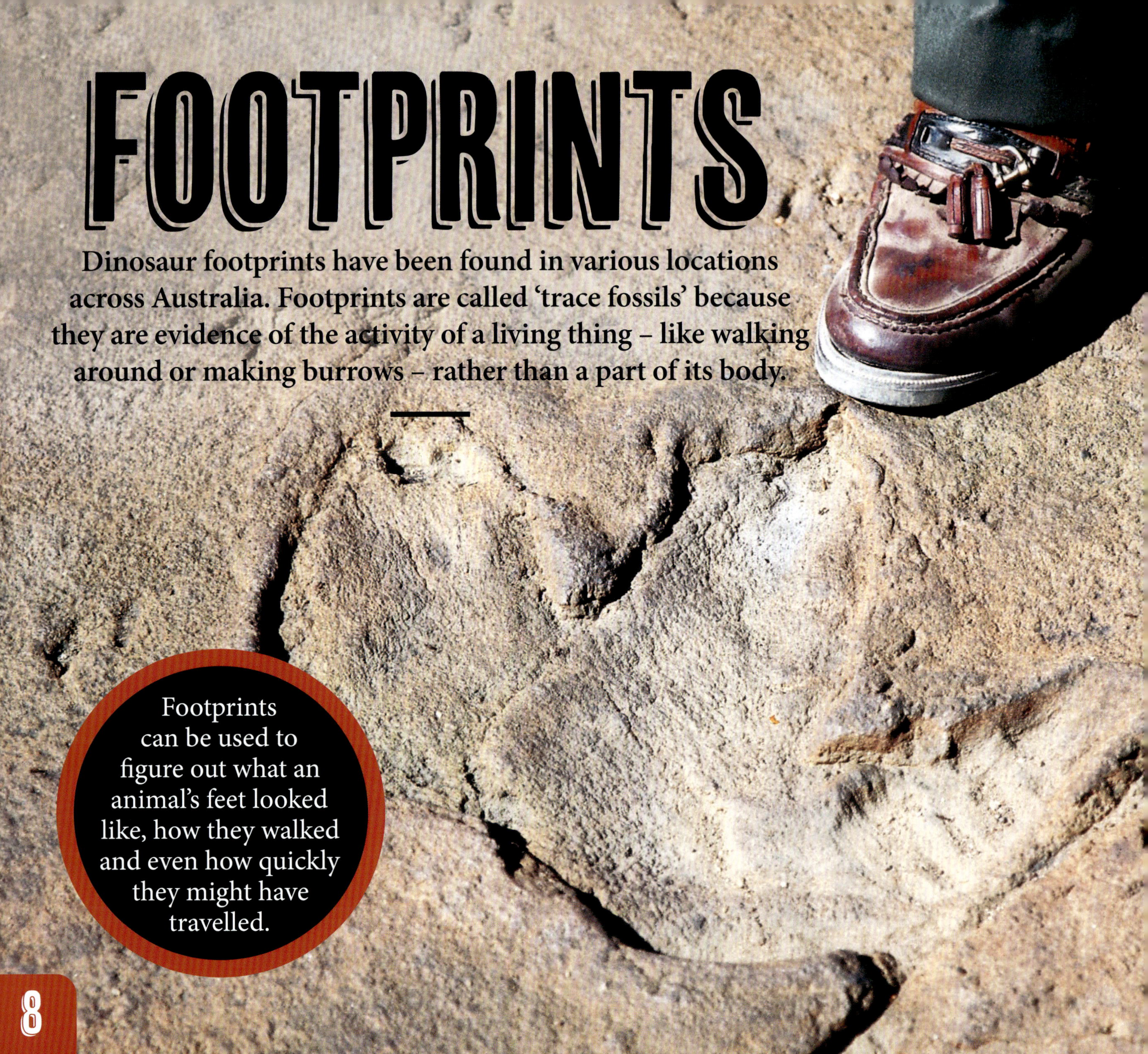

FOOTPRINTS

Dinosaur footprints have been found in various locations across Australia. Footprints are called 'trace fossils' because they are evidence of the activity of a living thing – like walking around or making burrows – rather than a part of its body.

Footprints can be used to figure out what an animal's feet looked like, how they walked and even how quickly they might have travelled.

Lark Quarry in Queensland is the site of more than 3000 footprints made by many different dinosaur species. For many years, scientists believed that this was evidence of a **STAMPEDE** that happened when a large dinosaur scared away a herd of smaller dinosaurs. Now palaeontologists think it is more likely that the footprints were made by travelling dinosaurs wading through shallow water.

A stretch of coastline on the Dampier Peninsula, WA, is home to thousands of tracks belonging to 21 different types of dinosaur. The area is sacred to the Goolarabooloo, who have known about the tracks for thousands of years. In Goolarabooloo **SONGLINES**, the three-toed tracks were made during the journey of a spirit-being called Marala – or 'Emu Man'.

THEROPOD ON THE HUNT

DID YOU KNOW?

During the 1990s, somebody carved out a dinosaur footprint from a sacred Indigenous site in Broome, WA. The thief was eventually caught, and the footprint was returned in 1998.

WHAT DID THEY LOOK LIKE?

TIMIMUS

The typical image that we have of dinosaurs – from things like movies and cartoons – is not always totally accurate. There are many surprising features of dinosaur bodies and we continue to discover more as we find more fossils.

FEATHERED FRIENDS

Feathers were first discovered on a dinosaur fossil in 1996 and since then we have found many more. Scientists have even used the fossils to figure out what colour the feathers on some dinosaurs might have been.

DID YOU KNOW?

Scientists have identified dinosaurs that were red, brown, orange, black, white and even shiny.

HEADBUTTERS AND HORN BLOWERS

Some dinosaurs had large crests and tubes on their heads, like a cassowary. Scientists still don't know what these were for, but they may have been used to butt heads or make noises.

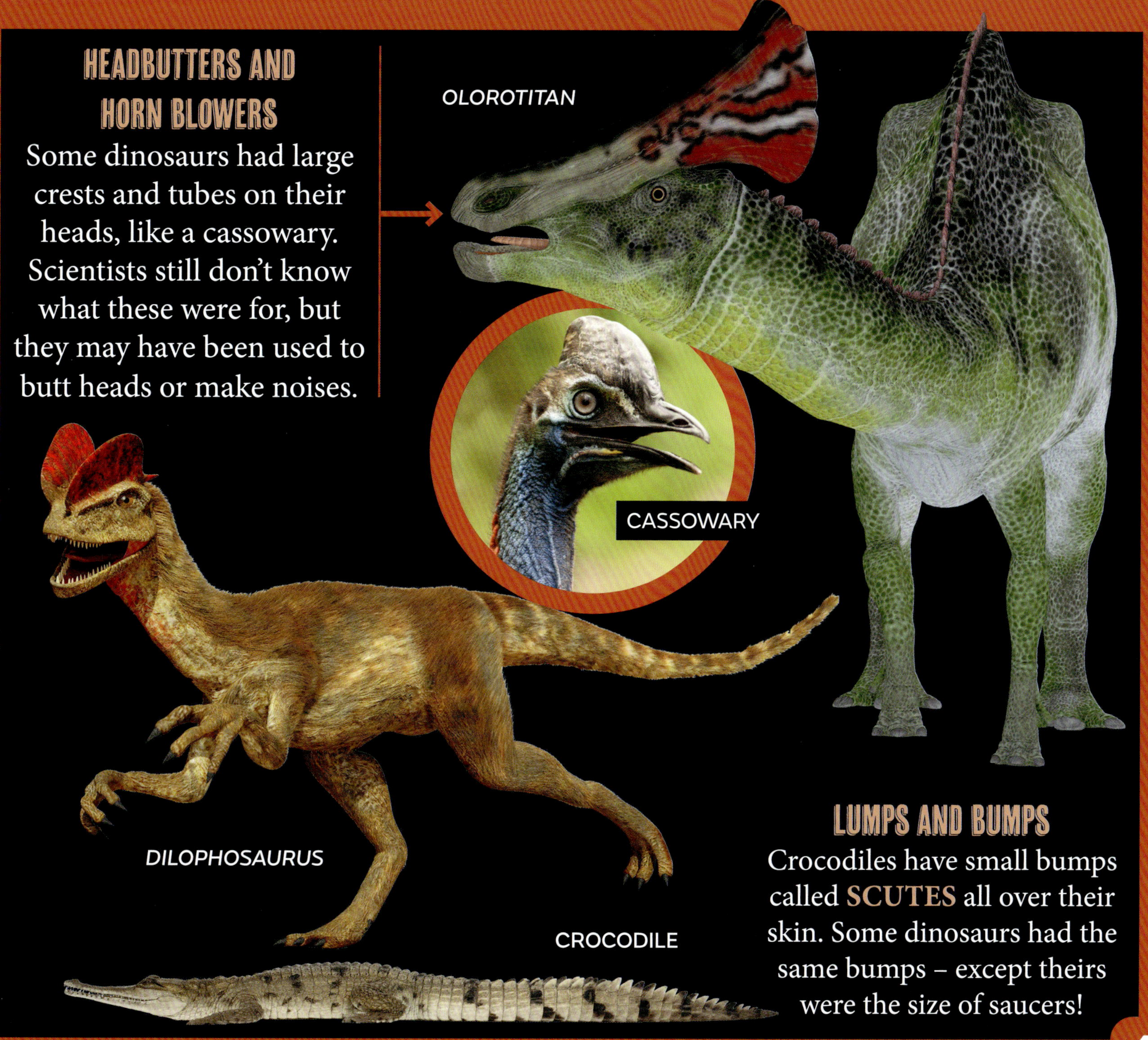

LUMPS AND BUMPS

Crocodiles have small bumps called **SCUTES** all over their skin. Some dinosaurs had the same bumps – except theirs were the size of saucers!

SAUROPODS

The largest dinosaur fossils ever found in Australia belong to sauropods. Sauropods were the largest animals ever to walk on Earth. Some grew up to 40m long.

These dinosaurs had very long necks that led to small heads, long tails and thick legs.

Sauropod species that lived in Australia include *Diamantinasaurus*, *Austrosaurus*, *Rhoetosaurus* and *Wintonotitan*.

DID YOU KNOW?

Sauropods walked on four legs and were herbivores. They had long, blunt teeth that could strip leaves from trees.

DIAMANTINASAURUS

The second-most complete sauropod skeleton found in Australia so far, *Diamantinasaurus* (nicknamed Matilda) was found in Winton in central Queensland.

DID YOU KNOW?

Matilda got its name from the song *Waltzing Matilda*!

The fossils were found in a 94-million-year-old **BILLABONG**. When Matilda lived, the area would have been very green, with lots of waterholes, lakes and different plants.

Matilda's real name is *Diamantinasaurus matildae*. Matilda was almost 16m long from its nose to the end of its tail. Its legs reached up to 2.5m high.

BONE FOSSILS OF MATILDA

THEROPODS

Theropods walked on two legs and were carnivores, which means they only ate meat. They had powerful legs and could run very quickly to catch their prey. The word theropod means 'beast-footed'.

TYRANNOSAURUS REX

Tyrannosaurus rex was a theropod that lived in North America.

Theropods had large, curved claws and sharp teeth and were vicious hunters. The bones in their hind legs were usually hollow, especially in smaller species.

Some scientists think *T. rex* would have been feathered!

DID YOU KNOW?

Research shows that today's birds have evolved from small theropod species.

Ceratosaurus, a theropod found in North America, had a horn on its snout and a smaller pair above its eyes.

AUSTRALOVENATOR

Australia's best-known carnivorous dinosaur skeleton is nicknamed Banjo, after the famous Australian bush poet, Banjo Paterson. This dinosaur's scientific name is *Australovenator wintonensis*.

Although it was fast, scientists believe that modern emus would be able to outrun this dinosaur.

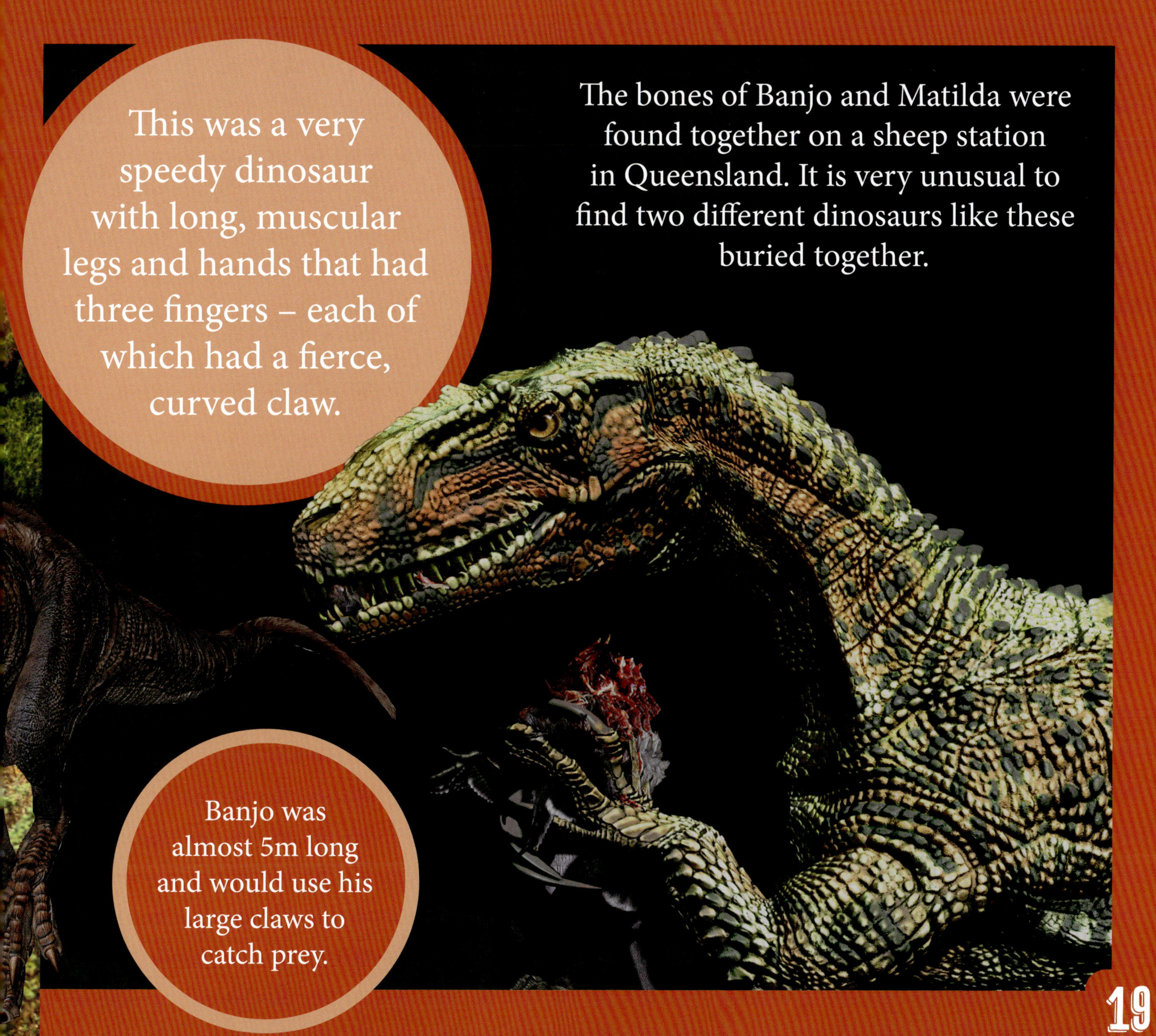

This was a very speedy dinosaur with long, muscular legs and hands that had three fingers – each of which had a fierce, curved claw.

The bones of Banjo and Matilda were found together on a sheep station in Queensland. It is very unusual to find two different dinosaurs like these buried together.

Banjo was almost 5m long and would use his large claws to catch prey.

ARMOURED DINOSAURS

Some dinosaurs had special armour on their bodies to protect them from larger meat-eating dinosaurs. The scientific name for this type of dinosaur is Thyreophorans, which means 'shield bearers'.

Armoured dinosaurs were herbivores and walked on four legs. The front pair of legs were shorter than the back pair.

STEGOSAURUS

One famous armoured dinosaur is *Stegosaurus*, which was a very large creature that mostly lived in North America. It could grow to 9m long – the length of a bus.

9 METRES

SMALL BRAIN

Despite their large, heavy bodies, these dinosaurs had brains that were only about the size of a walnut!

Many armoured dinosaurs had a club-like tail that could swing like a hammer – a useful weapon against **PREDATORS**.

TALARURUS

KUNBARRASAURUS

Kunbarrasaurus was an armoured dinosaur found in Queensland. It had armoured plates around its neck, as well as on its back and stomach. It also had spikes around its hips and tail.

KUNBARRASAURUS SKULL

Many pieces of the *Kunbarrasaurus* dinosaur were found, including an almost-whole skull, back bones, most of the left shoulder and arm, and armour plates. Even the contents of its stomach remained, which helped scientists figure out what it liked to eat.

This dinosaur grew to 3m long and 1m high, and could weigh up to 100kg.

DID YOU KNOW?

Kunbarra means 'shield' in the local Indigenous language where the fossils of this dinosaur were found.

ORNITHOPODS

Ornithopods were medium to large dinosaurs that had beaks and multiple rows of teeth. All ornithopods were herbivores and had the unique ability to chew their food – most reptiles simply gulp their food down.

DID YOU KNOW?
Ornithopods often moved in herds, for safety.

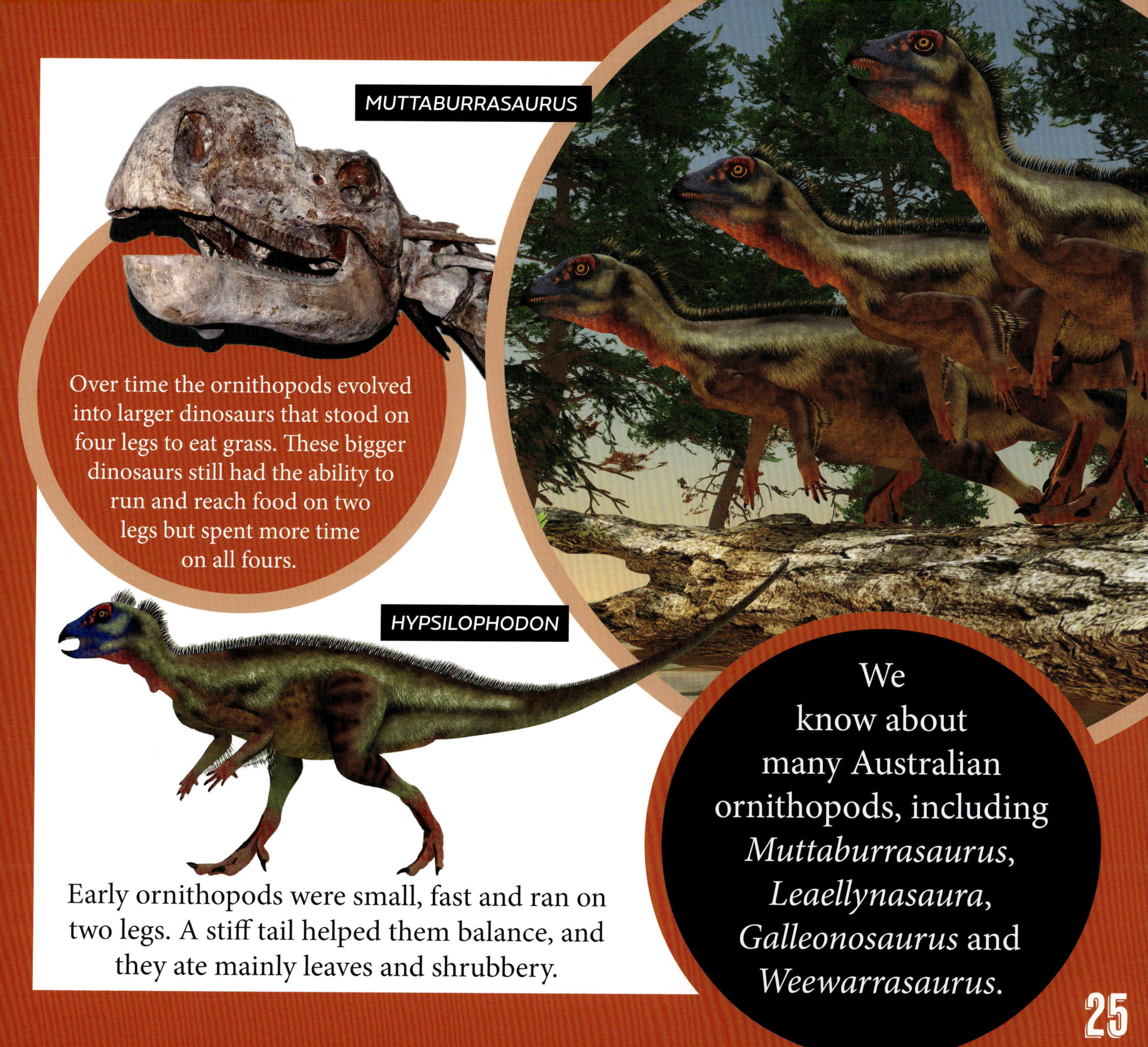

Over time the ornithopods evolved into larger dinosaurs that stood on four legs to eat grass. These bigger dinosaurs still had the ability to run and reach food on two legs but spent more time on all fours.

Early ornithopods were small, fast and ran on two legs. A stiff tail helped them balance, and they ate mainly leaves and shrubbery.

We know about many Australian ornithopods, including *Muttaburrasaurus*, *Leaellynasaura*, *Galleonosaurus* and *Weewarrasaurus*.

LEAELLYNASAURA

When this dinosaur was alive, Australia was located much closer to Antarctica than it is today and was very cold in the southern parts. This is where *Leaellynasaura* roamed, in temperatures between –2 °C and 5 °C.

The *Leaellynasaura* fossils were found at a place called Dinosaur Cove in Victoria.

Leaellynasaura had large eyes, which might have helped it to see in low light conditions. This would have been helpful in long, dark polar winters. It may have also had a furry or feathery coat to keep warm.

DID YOU KNOW?

Leaellynasaura grew to 1.5m long, although most of this length came from its tail, which was more than twice the length of its body.

A skull of this small dinosaur was found in Victoria by palaeontologists Patricia Vickers-Rich and Tom Rich, who named the species after their daughter.

FLYING AND SWIMMING REPTILES

PTERANODON

Many other reptiles lived in Australia when dinosaurs ruled the Earth, including flying reptiles, and swimming reptiles such as plesiosaurs, ichthyosaurs and mosasaurs.

Flying reptiles that lived at the same time as the dinosaurs were called pterosaurs. Like the marine reptiles, pterosaurs were not actually dinosaurs.

Pterosaur bones have been found in Queensland, Victoria, New South Wales and Western Australia.

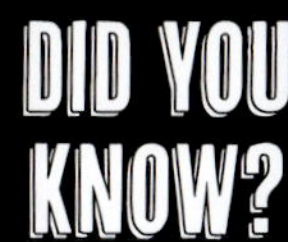

DID YOU KNOW?

The plesiosaur *Kronosaurus* could grow up to 10m in length.

Pterosaurs had strong powerful wings, so they could soar through the sky like birds. Scientists think pterosaurs lived near the sea and ate fish.

Kronosaurus was the largest marine reptile to swim in the ancient seas of inland Australia.

SHORT-TAILED PTEROSAUR

KRONOSAURUS

GLOSSARY

BILLABONG
A pool or stream of water that flows away from a river and leads nowhere else, like a cul-de-sac.

CRETACEOUS PERIOD
A time period that began 145 million years ago and ended 66 million years ago.

FOSSILS
The remains of animals or plants that died a very long time ago.

PREDATORS
Animals that hunt, kill, and eat other animals.

SCUTES
A bony plate that forms on an animal's skin.

SONGLINES
Ancient stories that explain the laws by which Indigenous people of the area live and how the land was created.

OPAL
A precious gem famous for its bright colours. Opal is Australia's national gemstone.

STAMPEDE
A sudden and panicked rush of a large group of animals.

WETLANDS
Areas where water covers the soil for all or part of the year, like swamps and marshes.

PICTURE CREDITS

Images are listed clockwise from top left unless specified otherwise.

AG = Australian Geographic; SS = Shutterstock.com; US = Unsplash.com; CP = CanvaPro

Front cover: Herschel Hoffmeyer/(SS); Mark Brandon/SS; Warpaint/SS; Marques/SS; Daniel Eskridge/SS; Daniel Eskridge/SS; Valentyna Chukhlyebova/SS; Valentyna Chukhlyebova/SS; Warpaint/SS; Daniel Eskridge/SS; Martin Leber/SS. **1:** dcwcreations/SS; Puwadol Jaturawutthichai/SS; Xing Lida/AG; Warpaint/SS. **2:** Xing Lida/AG. **3:** Linda Bucklin/SS; Daniel Eskridge/SS. **4:** Frances Mocnik/AG; Mircogen/SS. **5:** John Pickrell/AG. **6:** Andrew Gregory/AG. **7:** Sergey Krasovskiy/Getty; Bob Smith/Australian Opal Centre. **8:** Peter Lik/TEQ. **9:** Xing Lida/AG. **10:** Tea Marklong/SS; Xing Lida/AG. **11:** Catmando/SS; David Bristow/AG; Andrew Burgess/SS; Dotted Yeti/SS. **12:** Herschel Hoffmeyer/SS. **13:** Daniel Eskridge/SS; SA Hocknull, MA White, TR Tischler, AG Cook et al./ doi:10.1371/journal.pone.0006190; Bob Orsillo/SS. **14:** Nick Rains/AG; Xing Lida/AG. **15:** Scott A. Hocknull, Matt A. White, Travis R. Tischler, Alex G. Cook, Naomi D. Calleja, Trish Sloan, David A. Elliott/https://doi.org/10.1371/journal.pone.0006190. **16:** Martina Badini/SS. **17:** Daniel Eskridge/SS; Herschel Hoffmeyer/SS; DM7/SS. **18:** Merlyn Cantwell/Getty; Xida Ling/AG. **19:** Matt A. White, Phil R. Bell, Alex G. Cook, David G. Barnes, Travis R. Tischler, Brant J. Bassam, David A. Elliott/http://journals.plos.org/plosone/article?id=10.1371/journal.pone.0137709. **20:** Warpaint/SS. **21:** Suwat Wongkham/SS; Serhiy Smirnov/SS; Alexapicso/SS; Ralf Juergen Kraft/SS. **22:** Xing Lida/AG. **23:** Lucy G. Leahey, Ralph E. Molnar, Kenneth Carpenter, Lawrence M. Witmer, Steven W. Salisbury/https://peerj.com/articles/1475. **24:** Daniel Eskridge/SS. **25:** Matt Martyniuk (Dinoguy2)/Wikimedia Commons; Catmando/SS; Catmando/SS. **26:** Xing Lida/AG. **27:** Xing Lida/AG; Steve Morton & Thomas Rich/Museums Victoria. **28:** Warpaint/SS. **29:** Jiang Hongyan/SS; Konstantin G/SS; Andreas Wolochow/SS. **30:** Andrej Antic/SS; Daniel Eskridge/SS. **31:** akemontree/SS. **Back cover:** Xing Lida/AG.

Australian Geographic

DISCOVER

Australian Geographic *Discover: Mega Dinosaurs* is published by Australian Geographic. All text is copyright © Australian Geographic and may not be reproduced without the written permission of the publishers.

First published in 2020, reprinted in 2023
© Australian Geographic Holdings Pty Ltd
52–54 Turner St, Redfern, NSW

editorial@ausgeo.com.au
australiangeographic.com.au

ISBN: 978-1-925847-78-9

Editor: Lauren Smith
Sub-editors: Rebecca Cotton, Peter Tuskan
Creative director: Mike Ellot
Senior Designer: Harmony Southern
Print production: Katrina O'Brien and Andy Franks

AUSTRALIAN GEOGRAPHIC
Managing Director: David Haslingden
Director of Content: Liz Ginis
Licensing and Publishing Manager: Tom Bates
Commercial Assistant: Felicity McManus

Printed in China by C & C Offset Printing Co. Ltd.
The paper in this book is FSC® certified. FSC® promotes environmentally responsible, socially beneficial and economically viable management of the world's forests.

BOOKS IN THIS SERIES

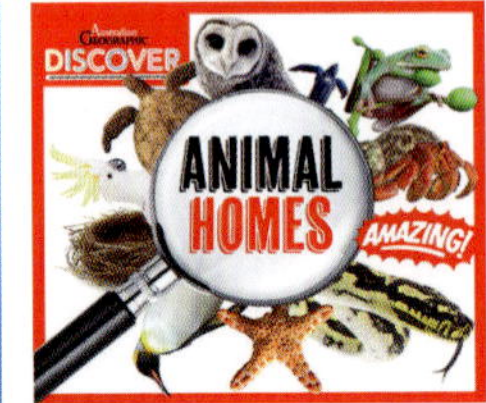

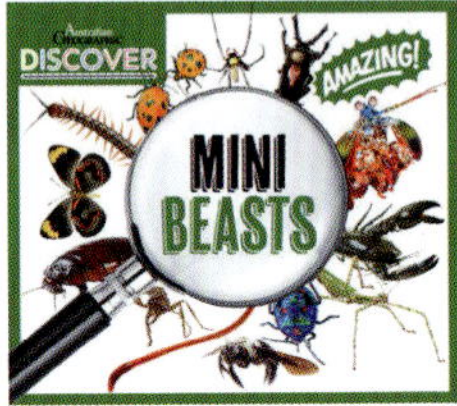

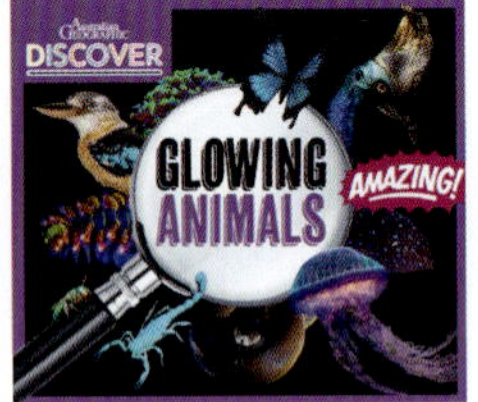

Australian Geographic contributes 100% of its profits to the Australian Geographic Society, including its conservation and sustainability programs.